# How to Create Powerful Mental Triggers

**GEO REPORT**
**2023**

# Preface

**Navigating the Future with Geo Report**

Dear reader,

It is with great pleasure that we welcome you to the world of technology, geospatial data analysis, and continuing education through this book. Here, you will come into contact with the most advanced concepts and the most up-to-date information in a constantly evolving scenario, guided by Geo Report, a company passionate about education and innovation.

Geo Report is much more than just a company; is a project whose mission is to illuminate the path of those who wish to explore the frontier of knowledge. Founded as an EdTech and GISTech, Geo Report offers services ranging from generating intelligence reports to producing educational resources that empower individuals and organizations to meet the challenges of the modern world.

**Geospatial Data Intelligence and Analysis Reports**: Imagine making strategic decisions based on accurate and up-to-date information. Geo Report uses cutting-edge technology to help companies and organizations transform geospatial data into valuable insights, providing significant competitive advantages.

**Continuing Education**: Learning is a never-ending journey, and Geo Report is committed to being your guide on this journey. Our books and educational materials promote both basic concepts and advanced knowledge about technology, supporting students, professionals and enthusiasts looking to improve and thrive in a world driven by innovation.

**Technological Update**: In the ever-changing world of technology, being out of date can be a critical disadvantage. Geo Report keeps a close eye on emerging technology trends and shares this information with you, ensuring you are always one step ahead.

This book is just one of the many tools Geo Report offers to enable you to navigate the vast ocean of technology. As you flip through these pages, you prepare to embark on a journey that will lead you to discover the power of geospatial data analysis, understand essential technology concepts, and stay up to date on the latest innovations.

As you dive into the content of this book, remember that Geo Report is at your side, ready to guide and support you in your quest for knowledge and technological excellence. The future is your blank canvas, and we're here to help you paint the brightest picture possible.

Happy studying and a learning journey full of discoveries!

Yours sincerely,

Geo Report Collaborators

# Chapter 1: Introduction to Mental Triggers

# 1. What are mental triggers?

What are mental triggers?

Mental triggers, also known as "psychological trigger" or "psychological trigger", are stimuli, words, images, situations or strategies that trigger specific responses in the human brain. They are elements that activate mental processes, often automatically and unconsciously, influencing a person's behavior, emotions and decisions. The psychological nature of mental triggers is deeply rooted in the understanding of human psychology and is explored in diverse areas, including marketing, persuasion, sales, social psychology, and user experience design.

Psychological Nature of Mental Triggers:

Mental triggers operate based on well-established psychological principles such as cognition, emotion and behavior. They explore tendencies inherent in the functioning of the human mind, such as the search for security, the need for belonging, the desire for novelty and loss aversion.

By activating these tendencies, mental triggers can influence people's decisions, often without them being aware of it.

Definition and Understanding in the Context of Human Behavior:

Mental triggers are, therefore, tools that exploit human psychology to create desired responses. They can be used to encourage the purchase of a product, promote subscription to a service, influence political opinions, encourage social actions and much more. To understand how mental triggers work, it is essential to understand how human beings process information, make decisions and respond to emotional stimuli.

Relevance in Various Areas:

Mental triggers are relevant in several areas of life, including:

1. Marketing and Advertising: Marketing strategies often rely on mental triggers to create attractive and persuasive advertisements.

2. Negotiation and Sales: Salespeople use mental triggers to influence buyers and close deals.

3. Social Psychology: Mental triggers are studied in social contexts to understand how people behave in groups.

4. User Experience Design (UX): In product and service design, mental triggers can improve usability and user retention.

5. Self-improvement: Individuals can use mental triggers to achieve personal goals, such as improving motivation and productivity.

Mental triggers are powerful elements that harness human psychology to influence our actions, thoughts and emotions. They play a fundamental role in many aspects of everyday life and are an important tool in fields involving persuasion and understanding human behavior.


## 2. The importance of mental triggers in marketing.

The Importance of Mental Triggers in Marketing:

Mental triggers play a vital role in the field of marketing, being a powerful tool for influencing and persuading consumers. Here are some key points that highlight its importance:

1. Influence on Purchasing Decisions: Consumers are inundated with information and choices every day. Mental triggers help direct people's attention to specific products, services or messages, making them stand out among the market noise.

2. Emotional Connection: Mental triggers have the ability to create an emotional connection with consumers. Purchasing decisions are often made based on emotions, and by incorporating emotional triggers, companies can create a stronger bond between brand and customer.

3. Acceleration of Decision Processes: Mental triggers can accelerate consumers' decision-making process. This is especially important in impulsive purchases, where the influence of the moment can be decisive.

4. Increased Conversion: The effective application of mental triggers in marketing campaigns can result in higher conversion rates, that is, more people who see the product or service become customers.

5. Retention and Loyalty: In addition to attracting new customers, mental triggers can also be used to maintain and retain existing customers. Strategies that emphasize reciprocity and ongoing value can strengthen brand ties.

Influence of Mental Triggers on Consumer Decisions:

Mental triggers influence consumer decisions by exploring fundamental aspects of human psychology. Some examples of how they affect decisions include:

1. Reciprocity: When a company offers something of value to consumers, such as a gift or useful content, consumers feel compelled to reciprocate, often purchasing products or services from the company.

2. Scarcity: The perception that something is scarce or limited in time can lead consumers to act quickly, fearing they will miss the opportunity.

3. Social Proof: When people see that others are satisfied with a product or service, they are more likely to follow suit as it creates a sense of trust and validation.

4. Authority: Demonstrating authority and expertise in a certain field can make consumers trust the company and its offerings more.

Examples of Companies or Campaigns that Benefited from Mental Triggers:

1. Amazon: Amazon uses mental scarcity triggers in its products, showing how many items are available in stock and how many have already been sold, encouraging buyers to act quickly.

2. Apple: Apple has built a brand around authority and innovation, convincing consumers that its products are the best and most advanced.

3. Booking.com: This hotel booking site uses scarcity and social proof, showing how many rooms are available and how many people are viewing a given hotel, encouraging quick booking.

4. Coca-Cola: Coca-Cola often creates emotional campaigns that appeal to nostalgia and emotions, connecting deeply with consumers.

Mental triggers play a vital role in marketing, influencing consumer decisions and increasing the effectiveness of marketing strategies. Companies that understand and apply these triggers effectively can achieve significant results in terms of customer acquisition and retention.


## 3. How mental triggers affect human behavior.


Mental triggers have the power to shape human behavior by exploring deep psychological principles inherent in human nature. They influence people's choices, decision-making and actions in many ways. Let's analyze in detail how mental triggers affect human behavior:

1. Reciprocity:
   - How it Works: The principle of reciprocity involves the human tendency to return favors and positive actions. When someone receives something, they feel compelled to give something in return.
   - Influence on Behavior: Companies that offer free samples, giveaways or useful content generally receive a positive response from customers, who feel inclined to purchase or engage more deeply with the brand.

- Example: Amazon offers related product suggestions based on customers' past purchases, using reciprocity to encourage more purchases.

2. Scarcity:
   - How it works: People tend to value more what is scarce or limited in time. Scarcity creates a sense of urgency.
   - Influence on Behavior: Limited-time promotions or products with limited stock often lead people to make purchasing decisions more quickly.
   - Example: Ticket sales for concerts or events often use scarcity as a tactic, announcing that "tickets are selling out quickly."

3. Social Prova:
   - How It Works: People have a tendency to follow the behavior of others when they are uncertain about what to do. Social proof involves influencing the actions and opinions of others.
   - Influence on Behavior: Customer reviews, testimonials and social media "like" counts are forms of social proof that can influence purchasing decisions and product choices.
   - Example: The Airbnb hosting platform displays reviews from other guests and the occupancy rate of properties, encouraging traveler confidence.

4. Authority:
   - How It Works: People tend to follow the lead of authority figures or experts in a certain field.
   - Influence on Behavior: Companies and individuals who demonstrate authority and knowledge on a subject are more likely to influence consumer decisions.
   - Example: The technology company Apple uses the prestige of its products and the image of Steve Jobs as a visionary leader to attract loyal followers.

5. Curiosity and FOMO (Fear of Missing Out):
   - How it Works: Curiosity is a human impulse to seek information and answers. FOMO is the fear of missing out on something important.
   - Influence Behavior: Marketing campaigns that generate curiosity or highlight unique opportunities can attract immediate attention and action.
   - Example: Netflix often releases series with exciting cliffhangers at the end of episodes, encouraging people to keep watching.

6. Emotions and Human Connection:
   - How it works: Emotions play a fundamental role in human decisions. People connect more deeply with emotional messages and stories.

- Influence on Behavior: Campaigns that evoke specific emotions can influence actions, such as donations to humanitarian causes.

- Example: Dove's women's self-esteem campaign, which promoted positive body image, connected emotionally with its audience.

These are just a few examples of how mental triggers have the power to influence human behavior. They explore fundamental aspects of human psychology to direct attention, create emotional connections, accelerate decisions, and encourage specific actions. Companies and marketers who understand and apply these principles can create more effective strategies to achieve their goals.

## 4. Psychological principles behind mental triggers.

Mental triggers are effective because of the fundamental psychological principles they explore. Let's explore some of these principles and how they relate to mental triggers:

1. Scarcity:

- Psychological Principle: The principle of scarcity is based on the human aversion to loss. People tend to value more what they perceive as rare or limited.
- Application to Mental Triggers: By creating a feeling of scarcity, mental triggers motivate people to act quickly, fearing losing the unique opportunity.

2. Reciprocity:
- Psychological Principle: Reciprocity is a widely accepted social norm. People feel a psychological obligation to reciprocate when someone gives them something.
- Application to Mental Triggers: When offering something of value, such as a gift, useful content or a favor, mental triggers stimulate reciprocity, making people more willing to respond positively.

3. Social Prova:
- Psychological Principle: People tend to follow the behavior of others when they are uncertain about what to do. Social conformity is an intrinsic part of human psychology.
- Application to Mental Triggers: By showing that others are using or endorsing a product or service, mental triggers use social proof to influence people's choices.

4. Authority:

- Psychological Principle: Respect for authority is a profound characteristic of human psychology. People are inclined to follow the lead of authority figures or experts.

- Application to Mental Triggers: By demonstrating authority in a certain field, whether through titles, awards or knowledge, mental triggers gain people's trust and influence them to follow.

5. Curiosity and FOMO (Fear of Missing Out):

- Psychological Principle: Curiosity is a motivating force that leads us to seek information and answers. FOMO is based on the fear of missing out on important opportunities.

- Application to Mental Triggers: Mental triggers explore curiosity by creating gaps in knowledge or highlighting unique opportunities, stimulating action based on the fear of missing something important.

6. Emotions and Human Connection:

- Psychological Principle: Emotions play a fundamental role in human decisions. Empathy and emotional connection are powerful elements of human psychology.

- Application to Mental Triggers: Mental triggers that evoke specific emotions can create a deeper connection with people, influencing their decisions and actions.

These psychological principles are deeply rooted in the understanding of human psychology and have been studied extensively. Mental triggers are strategies that capitalize on these principles to persuade and influence people in an ethical and effective way. By understanding how these principles work, companies and marketers can create more impactful strategies to achieve their goals while respecting the psychology and well-being of individuals.

5. Examples of effective mental triggers.

Certain mental triggers have been shown to be effective in different situations and contexts. Below are some concrete examples of mental triggers and how they have been successfully applied in different areas:

1. Reciprocity:
    - Example: Amazon offers free shipping on purchases over a certain value. This makes customers feel inclined to buy more products to enjoy the benefit.

2. Scarcity:
   - Example: Hotel booking sites often show how many rooms are available and how many people are viewing a given listing, creating a sense of scarcity and urgency.



3. Social Prova:
   - Example: Customer reviews on shopping sites such as Amazon significantly influence purchasing decisions. Shoppers are more likely to choose products with positive reviews.

4. Authority:
   - Example: Pharmaceutical companies often use the image of doctors and scientists in their advertising campaigns to convey authority and confidence in their products.

5. Curiosity and FOMO (Fear of Missing Out):
   - Example: Apple is known for its launch strategies, generating curiosity with cryptic ads and teasers that make people eager to see new products.

6. Emotions and Human Connection:

- Example: Dove's "Real Beauty" campaign challenged conventional beauty standards and evoked positive emotions, creating a deep emotional connection with its audience.

7. Reciprocity and Sales:
   - Example: During the holiday season, physical stores often offer product tastings, such as chocolates or drinks, creating a sense of reciprocity that leads customers to purchase gifts.

8. Shortage in Online Sales:
   - Example: Online stores often display messages such as "Only X units left" or "Offer valid today only", encouraging visitors to complete the purchase immediately.

9. Social Proof in Digital Marketing:
   - Example: Social networks often show the number of followers or likes on pages and posts, taking advantage of social proof to attract more followers.

10. Education Authority:
    - Example: Universities often highlight the academic credentials of their professors and researchers in their marketing campaigns, emphasizing authority in the educational field.

These examples illustrate how mental triggers can be adapted for different goals and industries. They are not restricted to marketing but are also widely applied in sales, education, psychology, policy and other fields. The versatility of mental triggers lies in their ability to tap into fundamental human psychology, influencing decisions and behaviors in a variety of contexts.

# Chapter 2: Authority and Credibility

# 1. The influence of authority on mental triggers.

The Influence of Authority on Mental Triggers:

Authority is a crucial component of mental triggers, and its influence is based on the psychological principle that people have an innate tendency to respect and follow the leadership of authority figures or experts in a given field. When applied as a mental trigger, authority can have a profound impact on people's decisions and actions.

How Perceived Authority Influences Decisions and Actions:

1. Credibility: Authority figures are seen as trustworthy and credible sources of information. The perception of credibility is fundamental to influencing people's decisions, as they tend to believe more in what is said by authorities compared to other sources.

2. Reduction of Uncertainty: The presence of authority reduces uncertainty in decisions. People feel more comfortable following guidance from

someone who demonstrates knowledge and expertise, as they believe this minimizes the risk of error.

3. Halo Effect: Authority in a specific area can "spread" its influence to other related areas. This is known as the halo effect, where trust in a specific field extends to other areas where authority is involved.

Examples of Leveraging Authority as a Mental Trigger:

1. Celebrity Endorsements: Many companies hire celebrities as ambassadors for their brands. These celebrities are seen as authorities in their fields and, by endorsing a product or service, can profoundly influence consumers' purchasing decisions.

2. Health Experts: Doctors and health experts are often used in advertising campaigns for health-related products. A doctor's authority can persuade people to follow treatment recommendations or choose certain medications.

3. Financial Professionals: Financial services companies often employ financial advisors with

certifications and experience in finance. This authority is used to persuade clients to make specific investment decisions.

4. Blogs and Online Content: Bloggers and influencers who establish themselves as authorities in specific niches can influence their followers' purchasing decisions. If they recommend products or services, their followers are more likely to consider those recommendations seriously.

5. Scientific and Academic Articles: Publishing scientific research in reputable journals or citing academic studies in persuasive arguments is a way to leverage intellectual authority.

These examples demonstrate how authority is an effective mental trigger in persuasion strategies. When people realize they are receiving advice or recommendations from an authoritative source, they are more likely to follow that guidance or take suggested actions. Authority is a powerful tool that can be used ethically to influence decisions in a variety of contexts.

## 2. Building your personal or business authority.

Building personal or business authority is a process that requires time, effort and consistency. Here are steps and strategies to help develop a solid, trustworthy reputation in a specific field:

1. Choose a Specific Niche or Topic:
   - Start by choosing a niche or topic where you want to build authority. Choosing a specific field allows you to focus on deepening your knowledge and experience.

2. Constantly Educate Yourself:
   - Stay up to date with the latest trends, research and developments in your field. Read books, articles, attend relevant courses and conferences, and follow influencers and experts in your niche.

3. Produce Quality Content:
   - Create valuable and informative content that helps others solve problems or gain knowledge. This can include blogs, videos, podcasts, webinars, academic articles, among others.

4. Share Your Knowledge:

- Don't be afraid to share what you know. Contribute to forums, discussion groups, social networks, and other communities related to your field. Answer questions, provide insights, and help others.

5. Develop Relationships:

- Connect with other professionals, influencers and peers in your field. Strong relationships can open doors to collaboration opportunities and increase your visibility.

6. Build a Solid Online Presence:

- Have a professional website and active profiles on relevant social networks. Make sure your content is consistent and aligns with your area of authority.

7. Publications and Presentations:

- Contribute articles to reputable publications in your niche. Additionally, consider giving talks or presentations at conferences and webinars to share your knowledge.

8. Demonstrate Consistency and Credibility:

- Meet deadlines, be reliable and maintain high ethical standards. Consistency over time is key to building a solid reputation.

9. Collection of Testimonials and Recommendations:

- Ask clients, colleagues or followers to provide testimonials or recommendations about your expertise and skills. This can be used as proof of your authority.

10. Learn from Feedback:

- Be open to constructive feedback and use it to improve. Show that you are willing to learn and grow in your field.

11. Be Patient:

- Building authority takes time. Don't expect instant results. Focus on your passion for the topic and the quality of your work.

12. Support Network:

- Building personal or business authority is often an easier journey when you have a support network. Talk to mentors, colleagues, and friends who can offer guidance and support along the way.

Remember that building authority is an ongoing process. As you become more recognized in your field, the responsibility for maintaining and enhancing your authority increases. Be authentic, committed, and dedicated to your niche, and you will see your authority gradually grow over time.

## 3. Testimonials and case studies as credibility tools.

Testimonials and Case Studies as Credibility Tools:

Testimonials and case studies are powerful tools for strengthening the credibility of an individual, company or product. They are used to demonstrate real results and positive experiences, which can positively impact other people's perceptions. Here are some ways to utilize them effectively:

Testimonials from Satisfied Customers:

1. Impact on Perception: Testimonials from satisfied customers provide social evidence of the quality of a product or service. They increase confidence in new customers by showing that others have had a positive experience.

2. Humanizing the Brand: Testimonials add a human dimension to your brand or company, showing that you are serving real people with real needs and challenges.

3. Relevance: Make sure testimonials are relevant to the target audience. Potential customers should identify with the testimonials and feel like their own concerns are being addressed.

Case studies:

1. Tangible Evidence: Case studies provide tangible evidence of how your product or service solved problems or achieved positive results for your customers.

2. Context and Depth: They allow you to tell the complete story, describing the initial challenge, the solutions adopted and the results achieved. This helps create an engaging narrative.

3. Demonstration of Experience: Case studies demonstrate your knowledge and expertise in your field. They show that you deeply understand your customers' problems and needs.

Guidelines for Collecting and Presenting Testimonials and Case Studies in a Compelling Manner:

1. Ask for Permission: Always ask customers for permission before using their testimonials or case studies. Make sure they are comfortable sharing their experiences.

2. Be Authentic: Do not alter or over-edit testimonials. They must reflect the real voice and experience of customers.

3. Include Tangible Data: In case studies, provide concrete numbers and metrics to illustrate success. This makes the results more convincing.

4. Use Visual Media: Add photos or videos of satisfied customers or completed projects whenever possible. Visual media makes stories more engaging.

5. Present Before and After: If applicable, show the situation before your product or service and how it improved after implementation.

6. Highlight Benefits and Results: Focus on the benefits customers gained from your help. This shows the real value you provide.

7. Be Transparent: Provide enough information so that people can understand the context of the testimonials or case studies. Transparency increases credibility.

8. Update Regularly: As you get more testimonials and case studies, update your presentations to keep the content relevant and current.

Using testimonials and case studies effectively requires an ethical and authentic approach. They are valuable tools for building credibility and gaining public trust, highlighting the real results you deliver to customers.

## 4. How to use certificates and seals of approval.

Importance of Certificates and Seals of Approval:

Certificates and seals of approval play a key role in building the credibility of an individual, company or product. They function as external indicators that certain quality, safety or compliance standards have been met. Their importance includes:

1. Consumer Confidence: Certificates and seals of approval increase consumer confidence by indicating that a product or service is trustworthy and meets certain criteria.

2. Market Differentiation: In competitive markets, certificates can differentiate a company or product, demonstrating its commitment to quality.

3. Legal Compliance: In some industries, compliance with specific regulations is mandatory. Certificates and seals guarantee that the company is compliant.

4. Attractiveness to Business Partners: Companies seeking partnerships or collaborations can benefit from displaying certifications that show their credibility.

5. Risk Reduction: Safety or quality assurance certificates can reduce legal and liability risks.

Types of Relevant Certificates and Seals:

The types of certificates and seals vary according to the industry and area of activity. Some examples include:

1. ISO Quality Certificates: ISO 9001 (quality management) and ISO 14001 (environmental management) certifications are widely recognized in various industries.

2. Food Safety Certificates: Such as the HACCP Certificate (Hazard Analysis and Critical Control Points) for food companies.

3. Professional Certifications: Certificates issued by professional organizations or associations, such as IT, medical, or legal certifications.

4. Internet Security Seals: Such as SSL (Secure Sockets Layer) for website security.

5. Consumer Seals of Approval: Granted by consumer protection organizations or product and service evaluations.

Tips for Obtaining and Displaying Certificates and Seals Effectively:

1. Identify Relevant Requirements: Find out which certificates and seals are most relevant to your industry or area of activity, considering regulations and market expectations.

2. Meet the Requirements: Make sure your company or product meets all the necessary requirements to obtain the desired certificates.

3. Research Reputable Certification Organizations: Choose certification organizations that are reputable and recognized in your industry.

4. Follow Display Guidelines: Respect the display guidelines for certificates and seals, ensuring they are presented clearly and legibly on your website, products or marketing materials.

5. Update Regularly: Keep your certificates up to date, renewing them as necessary. Displaying expired certificates can damage credibility.

6. Communicate Transparently: Provide clear information about what certificates mean and how they benefit your customers or partners.

7. Use Case Studies: In addition to simply displaying certificates, share case studies or success stories that highlight how certificates have contributed to the quality or safety of your products or services.

8. Evaluate Customer Feedback: Listen to customer feedback to ensure your products or services are up to the standards indicated by the certificates.

9. Training and Awareness: Ensure your staff are aware of the standards and regulations associated with certificates and seals and receive appropriate training if necessary.

Certificates and seals of approval are valuable credibility assets that can help build trust with your customers and partners. They must be used ethically and transparently to maximize their benefits.

## 5. Strategies for demonstrating expertise.

Demonstrating expertise in a given field is essential to building credibility and standing out. Here are practical strategies to achieve this:

1. Continuing Education:
   - Seek ongoing education and training in your field. Certifications, online courses, workshops and participation in conferences are ways to stay up to date.

2. Publishing Quality Content:
   - Create and regularly share relevant and valuable content, such as articles, blogs, videos or podcasts, that showcases your knowledge and experience.

3. Social Media and Blogging:
   - Use social media platforms and blogs to share information and insights related to your field. Participate in relevant discussions and groups.

4. Lectures and Presentations:
   - Offer lectures, webinars and presentations at conferences or events related to your area of expertise.

5. Collaborations and Partnerships:

- Collaborate with other respected professionals in your field for joint projects, articles or research.

6. Mentoring:
   - Offer to mentor newer professionals in your field, sharing your knowledge and guiding them.

7. Publications and Recognition in Reputable Media:
   - Seek opportunities to be quoted in reputable media, such as newspapers, magazines and news websites.

8. Development of Tools and Resources:
   - Create helpful tools, guides, templates, or resources that demonstrate your practical knowledge.

9. Participation in Committees and Professional Associations:
   - Be active in committees or professional associations related to your field, showing your commitment to excellence.

10. Satisfied Customers and Case Studies:
   - Present testimonials from satisfied customers and case studies that highlight how your expertise solved problems or generated positive results.

11. Thought Leadership:
   - Assume a thought leadership position in your field by expressing innovative opinions and perspectives.

Examples of Individuals and Companies that Have Demonstrated Expertise:

1. Elon Musk (Tesla and SpaceX): Musk is widely recognized as an expert in space technology and electric vehicles due to the success of his companies, SpaceX and Tesla.

2. Neil deGrasse Tyson (Astrophysicist): Tyson is a science communicator who has demonstrated expertise in astrophysics through his television programs, books and lectures.

3. Harvard Business Review: The Harvard Business Review is a publication that attracts business experts and thought leadership to write articles about trends and challenges in the business world.

4. HubSpot (Digital Marketing): HubSpot is a digital marketing company that demonstrates expertise in inbound marketing and marketing automation,

sharing educational resources and offering certifications.

5. Dr. Anthony Fauci (Infectious Disease Expert): Fauci has demonstrated expertise in infectious diseases and led public health efforts during the COVID-19 pandemic.

These examples illustrate how individuals and companies can stand out by demonstrating expertise in their fields. The combination of ongoing education, knowledge sharing, and thought leadership is essential to building and maintaining authority in a specific field.

# Chapter 3: Scarcity and Urgency

# 1. How scarcity influences decisions.

Scarcity is a powerful psychological factor that affects people's decisions in many ways. It is based on the idea that human beings tend to value more that which is perceived as rare, limited or difficult to obtain. Here are some key concepts related to scarcity and how it influences decisions:

1. Fear of Missing Opportunities (FOMO - Fear of Missing Out):
   - People are afraid of losing unique or advantageous opportunities. When something is perceived as scarce, the fear of missing the chance to obtain it often drives action.

2. Valuation of Rare Items:
   - Rare items or resources are often perceived as more valuable. Scarcity increases the perceived value of an item, even if its intrinsic value is the same.

3. Sense of Urgency:

- Scarcity creates a sense of urgency, prompting people to act quickly to acquire what is missing before it is too late.

4. Influence on Purchasing Decisions:

- In the context of shopping, scarcity can lead people to purchase products or services that they might not otherwise purchase, simply because they believe the supply is limited in time or quantity.

Research and Studies on the Influence of Scarcity:

1. Chocolate Cookie Experiment (Worchel et al., 1975): This classic study involved the presentation of chocolate cookies in two situations: one in which cookies were plentiful and one in which they were scarce. The results showed that scarce cookies were rated as tastier and more desirable, even though they were identical to abundant cookies.

2. Flash Sales and Time-Limited Offers: Many companies use flash sales strategies and limited-time offers to take advantage of the scarcity principle. Consumers are encouraged to purchase products or services based on the perception that the offer is temporary.

3. Online Auction Strategies: Online auction sites like eBay make use of scarcity by showing how many items are available and how much time is left to bid. This creates competition between buyers and can result in higher bids.

4. Limited Product Releases (e.g., Limited Edition): Many companies release products in limited editions to create a sense of scarcity. This not only attracts consumers, but can also lead to these products being resold at higher prices due to their perceived rarity.

These studies and examples demonstrate that scarcity is a powerful psychological influence that can shape human behavior and significantly affect purchasing decisions. People tend to value more what is scarce, which leads them to act differently than they would in situations of abundance. Understanding this principle is critical for marketers and salespeople who want to create effective persuasive strategies.

## 2. Scarcity creation strategies in marketing.

Scarcity Creation Strategies in Marketing:

Creating scarcity is an effective marketing strategy for stimulating demand and driving sales. Here are some common tactics that can be used to create a sense of scarcity:

1. Limited Stocks:
- Announcing that there are only a limited number of products available can encourage consumers to act quickly so as not to miss the opportunity. For example, "Only 10 units left!"

2. Exclusive Limited Time Offers:
- Offering discounts, promotions or special packages for a limited period can create a sense of urgency. For example, "50% discount today only!"

3. Limited Releases:
- Launching products or special editions in limited quantities generates interest and desire. This is often seen in sneaker, clothing, and collectible releases.

4. Countdown:
- Using a countdown timer on your website or in email campaigns can create a sense of urgency, encouraging customers to take action before time runs out.

5. Exclusive Pre-sale:

   - Offering an exclusive pre-sale to a select group of customers or email subscribers can create a sense of privilege and scarcity.

6. Limited Supply by Region:

   - Limiting the availability of a product or service to certain regions or countries can create a geographic scarcity, encouraging people in those areas to take action.

7. Flash Promotions:

   - Running flash promotions, in which a product is offered at a very reduced price for a short period, can attract immediate buyers.

8. "Last Chance" and "Running Out Quickly":

   - Using phrases like "Last chance to buy" or "Running out quickly" in your ads or product descriptions creates a sense of urgency.

9. Limited Time Offers on Online Shopping:

   - Online shopping sites often use countdown timers to show how long an item will be available at a promotional price.

10. Limited Registration for Webinars or Events:
   - Limiting the number of seats at webinars, online seminars, or live events can create a shortage of participation.


Ethical and Effective Use of Scarcity in Marketing:

Creating scarcity is an effective strategy when used ethically. It is important not to mislead customers by creating false shortages. Here are some guidelines:

1. Transparency: Be transparent about the details of the shortage. Inform customers of actual available quantities or actual deadlines.

2. Meet Deadlines: Make sure limited-time offers actually expire when promised. Don't artificially extend promotions.

3. Communicate the Reason: Explain why the shortage exists. It could be due to a limited edition, low stock or seasonality.

4. Create Real Value: Make sure the offer in question really has value for customers. Don't use scarcity as a tactic to push unwanted products.

5. Evaluate Feedback: Be open to customer feedback to understand how they perceive your scarcity strategies.

Scarcity is a valuable tool when used ethically, as it can boost customer engagement, increase sales, and create an exciting shopping experience.

3. Using limited-time promotions.
Limited Time Promotions to Create Urgency:

Limited-time promotions are a common marketing tactic to create urgency for consumers to act. They work by establishing a clear deadline during which consumers can take advantage of a discount, special offer or additional benefit. Here are the details on how effective this strategy is:

1. Creating Urgency: By setting a deadline, limited-time promotions create a sense of urgency. Consumers feel they need to act quickly to take advantage of the offer before it expires.

2. Generating Excitement: Limited-time promotions generate excitement and anticipation among consumers as they anticipate a significant reward or savings.

3. Quick Decision Making: Urgency induces consumers to make purchasing decisions more quickly. This can speed up the purchasing process.

Guidelines for Planning and Executing Limited-Time Promotions:

1. Set Clear Objectives: Set specific goals for the promotion, such as increasing sales, clearing inventory or acquiring new customers.

2. Determine the Deadline: Carefully choose the promotion period. The deadline should be short enough to create urgency, but not so short that it discourages participation.

3. Communicate in Advance: Announce the promotion in advance to create anticipation. Use emails, social media, website and other channels to inform customers about the upcoming offer.

4. Offer Real Value: Make sure the promotion offers real value to customers. Significant discounts,

freebies or additional benefits are effective ways to attract consumers.

5. Create Attractive Marketing Assets: Develop eye-catching marketing materials such as banners, ads and images that highlight the promotion and deadline.

6. Track Results: Use analysis tools to track promotion performance. This allows you to adjust future strategies based on real data.

7. Understand Legal Limitations: Be aware of advertising and sales regulations in your market. Certain terms and conditions may be mandatory.

Benefits and Challenges of Limited Time Promotions:

Benefits:

1. Increased Sales: Limited-time promotions can significantly increase sales during the promotion period.

2. Stock Clearance: These promotions are effective for selling in-stock or seasonal products.

3. Acquisition of New Customers: Urgency can attract new customers who were considering making a purchase.

Challenges:

1. Discount Margins: Offering discounts can affect profit margins, especially if not well planned.

2. Future Expectations: Customers can expect regular promotions, making it harder to sell at full price.

3. Communication Overload: If not managed properly, constant communication about promotions can be irritating for customers.

Limited-time promotions are a powerful tool for creating urgency in consumers' purchasing decisions. When planned and executed carefully, they can increase sales and customer engagement. However, it is important to balance the benefits with the challenges associated with this strategy.

## 4. Scarcity of products and limited edition.

Limited Edition and Generating Exclusive Interest:

Offering limited edition products is a powerful marketing strategy that generates unique interest and demand among consumers. It is based on perceived scarcity, where customers know there are only a limited number of items available for a short period. Here is a breakdown of this strategy:

1. Creating Exclusivity: Limited edition products create a feeling of exclusivity, as consumers realize that they are purchasing something unique and rare.

2. Urgency and Purchasing Impulse: The limited nature of the supply creates urgency, prompting consumers to act quickly to purchase the product before it runs out.

3. Customer Loyalty: Customers may feel more inclined to purchase limited edition products from a brand they value, thus strengthening brand loyalty.

4. Generating Zeal and Hype: Limited edition products often generate excitement on social media and in the community, creating zeal and hype around the brand.

Success Stories of Limited Edition Brands:

1. Nike: Nike is known for its limited-edition collaborations with designers and celebrities. Nike's limited edition sneakers, like Air Jordan models, often sell out quickly due to high demand and exclusive appeal.

2. Apple: Apple launched limited edition products, such as the iPhone RED, in partnership with (RED) to support the fight against AIDS. These products generate excitement and contribute to a good cause.

3. Hermès: The luxury brand Hermès is known for its limited edition bags, such as the Birkin and Kelly. The scarcity of these bags adds to their aura of exclusivity and desirability.

Adequate Production and Distribution Management:

Properly managing the production and distribution of scarce products is crucial to the success of this strategy:

1. Advance Planning: Forecast demand and plan production in advance, taking into account manufacturing and delivery time.

2. Clear Communication: Inform customers of the launch date and number of units available. Clear communication helps create expectations.

3. Pre-sale and Reservations: Consider the pre-sale option to gauge demand in advance and ensure you have enough products.

4. Real-Time Monitoring: Constantly monitor stock levels during the limited edition period and report any imminent stock-outs.

5. Development of Marketing Strategies: Create compelling marketing strategies that highlight the exclusivity and urgency of the limited edition.

6. Geographic Exclusivity: If desired, limit availability geographically to create a sense of scarcity in specific regions.

7. Customer Service: Be prepared to handle customer questions and concerns about product availability.

Effective use of limited edition products can strengthen your brand, increase sales, and create excitement among customers. However, it is important to carefully manage production and distribution to avoid frustration and ensure that the strategy is perceived as authentic and valuable by consumers.

## 5. Psychology of urgency and how to apply it.

Emergency Psychology:

The psychology of urgency is based on the idea that human beings are influenced by a sense of rush and the need to make quick decisions. This occurs because urgency activates our survival instinct and makes us act to avoid loss or take advantage of an opportunity. Here are the main elements of the psychology of urgency:

1. Fear of Missing Out: People are afraid of losing opportunities, resources or benefits. When they realize something is about to disappear, they feel the pressure to act quickly to avoid losing it.

2. Sense of Scarcity: The perception that something is limited or scarce increases its perceived value.

This is because scarcity makes us believe that something is more valuable because of its rarity.

3. Sense of Opportunity: Urgency creates a sense of unique opportunity. People feel like they are getting something special or exclusive when they act quickly.

Application of Urgency:

Urgency can be applied in different ways in different contexts, such as sales, online marketing and negotiations. Here are some ways to apply it effectively:

1. Limited Time Promotions: Offer discounts or special offers for a limited period of time. Clearly communicate the expiration date to create urgency.

2. Countdown: Use countdown timers on your website to show how long customers have to take advantage of an offer or make a purchase.

3. Limited Stock: Advertise limited product stocks to encourage customers to act quickly before the item runs out.

4. Exclusivity: Offer exclusive access to a select group of customers for a limited time, creating a sense of privilege.

5. Online Auctions: Use time-bound online auctions to create competition among participants and encourage higher bids.

6. Progressive Discounts: Offer progressive discounts that decrease as time passes, encouraging immediate purchases.

7. Flash Deals: Announce surprise offers for a short period of time, surprising customers with an unexpected opportunity.

Effective Emergency Communication:

To effectively communicate urgency to consumers or stakeholders, follow these guidelines:

1. Be Clear and Transparent: Communicate the conditions and limitations of the offer clearly and transparently to avoid misunderstandings.

2. Highlight Scarcity: Emphasize that the supply is limited in quantity, time or geographic availability.

3. Use Persuasive Language: Use persuasive words and phrases, such as "last chance", "limited stock" and "exclusive offer".

4. Show Clear Benefits: Explain the benefits customers will gain by acting quickly.

5. Use Visual Elements: In addition to text, use visual elements like countdown graphics to reinforce urgency.

6. Promote on Social Media: Use social media to build anticipation and inform followers about the rush offer.

7. Send Reminders: Send email reminders or notifications to alert customers about the offer expiration date.

8. Test and Measure: Try different urgency approaches and measure the results to identify the most effective strategies.

Applying the psychology of urgency can be a persuasive and effective strategy in various contexts. However, it is important to use it ethically and transparently to build trust with customers and avoid creating a feeling of excessive pressure.

# Chapter 4: Reciprocity and Giving before Receiving

# 1. The principle of reciprocity.

Principle of Reciprocity:

The principle of reciprocity is a fundamental psychological phenomenon that describes the human tendency to respond to one favorable action with another favorable action. In other words, when someone does us a favor, gives us something, or acts generously toward us, we feel an unconscious obligation to reciprocate in some way. This principle is an essential part of social interactions and has a profound impact on human behavior.

Influence of Reciprocity on Human Behavior and Social Interactions:

Reciprocity influences human behavior in several ways:

1. Creation of Social Bonds: Reciprocity strengthens social bonds by creating a mutual exchange of benefits. This helps to establish trust and solidarity in interpersonal relationships.

2. Strengthening Cooperation: The expectation of reciprocity encourages people to cooperate with each other. Knowing that their positive actions will be reciprocated, people have an incentive to work together constructively.

3. Conflict Resolution: Reciprocity can be used to resolve conflicts and disputes. When one party acts generously or makes concessions, the other party tends to respond in a similar way, facilitating resolution.

4. Marketing and Sales: The principle of reciprocity is widely used in marketing and sales strategies. Companies offer giveaways, free samples or discounts to create a sense of obligation in customers, encouraging purchase.

5. Altruistic Help: Reciprocity is also related to altruistic help. When someone receives help in a time of need, they are more likely to be willing to help others in similar situations.

Studies and Examples of Reciprocity:

1. Free Gifts Study (Regan, 1971): In this classic study, participants were asked to help an experimenter with a task. Then, the experimenter

"presented" the participants with a soft drink. Later, when participants had the opportunity to reciprocate, those who received the gift were more likely to help again than those who received nothing.

2. Free Samples in Supermarkets: Many supermarkets offer free product samples to customers. These samples are given with the expectation that customers will purchase the product later.

3. Crowdfunding Campaigns: In crowdfunding campaigns, creators often offer rewards to supporters. These rewards exploit the principle of reciprocity to encourage contributions.

4. Giveaways at Marketing Events: At marketing events, such as trade shows, companies often give out giveaways, such as personalized pens or bags, to attract visitors and potential customers.

These examples illustrate how people tend to respond positively when something is given to them, creating a sense of obligation to give back in some way. The principle of reciprocity plays a significant role in our social and economic lives, shaping our interactions and influencing our decisions.

## 2. How to offer value before asking for something.

Offering Value Before Asking:

Offering value before requesting something from others is a fundamental strategy for building solid relationships, both personal and professional. This approach demonstrates consideration, empathy and respect for others, creating an environment conducive to strengthening connections and building trust.

Importance of Offering Value Before Asking:

1. Building Trust: By offering value initially, you demonstrate that you are willing to invest in the relationship and that you are not just interested in personal benefits. This helps build mutual trust.

2. Creating Lasting Relationships: Relationships based on reciprocity and the mutual offering of value tend to be more lasting and meaningful.

3. Strengthening Reputation: Acting generously and providing assistance to others contributes to a good reputation and is often rewarded with respect and admiration.

4. Facilitating Partnerships and Collaborations: When you offer value before asking, others are more likely to be willing to collaborate and partner with you.

Strategies for Offering Value Before Asking:

1. Share Knowledge: Proactively offer your knowledge and experience, whether through mentoring, lectures, workshops or practical tips.

2. Help without Expectations: Be willing to help others without expecting anything in return. This demonstrates your genuine concern for their well-being.

3. Be a Good Listener: Listen carefully to the needs and concerns of those around you and offer support or advice when appropriate.

4. Be Available: Be available to help whenever necessary, demonstrating that you value the time and needs of others.

5. Introduce Connections: Make introductions between people who can benefit from each other, creating opportunities for both.

Benefits of Offering Value:

1. Building Solid Networks: Offering value creates a robust and reliable network of contacts, which can be beneficial in times of need.

2. Community Strengthening: By contributing to the well-being of your community or work environment, you help create a more positive and collaborative environment.

3. Development of Social Skills: Practicing generosity and offering value improves your social skills and empathy.

4. Increased Professional Opportunities: Solid relationships can result in new professional opportunities, such as jobs, collaborative projects or recommendations.

5. Personal Satisfaction: The feeling of making a difference in someone's life and being appreciated for it contributes to personal satisfaction and emotional well-being.

Offering value before asking for something is a strategy that enriches relationships, builds trust and creates opportunities in an ethical and lasting way. Remember that genuine generosity and concern for the well-being of others are the foundations of this approach.

## 3. Giveaway and free sample strategies.

Free Gift and Sample Strategies:

Offering free gifts and samples is an effective strategy for applying the principle of reciprocity in marketing and attracting customers. Here are some strategies for implementing this tactic effectively:

1. Audience Segmentation: Identify your target audience and their interests to offer freebies or samples that are relevant to them. This increases the likelihood that customers will appreciate the gesture.

2. Special Promotions: Associate the distribution of gifts or free samples with special promotions, such as a discount on your first purchase or an exclusive offer. This creates a sense of additional value.

3. Loyalty Programs: Create loyalty programs that reward customers with free gifts or samples after a specific number of purchases or points accumulated.

4. Events and Trade Shows: Distribute giveaways and samples at events, trade shows and exhibitions related to your industry. This attracts potential customers interested in your product or service.

5. Incorporation into Purchases: Include gifts or free samples with high-value purchases or service subscriptions, encouraging customers to choose more comprehensive packages.

6. Referral Programs: Reward customers who refer new customers with free gifts or samples. This motivates current customers to promote your brand.

7. Customized Samples: Offer customized samples based on customer preferences, demonstrating that you value their individual choices.

Common Use in Marketing:

Distributing gifts and free samples is a widely used marketing tactic to attract customers and retain them. Here are some common ways to apply this strategy:

1. Product Samples: Many companies offer free samples of their products to allow customers to try before they buy. This is common in industries such as beauty, food and beverage.

2. Promotional Gifts: Companies often distribute personalized gifts, such as pens, t-shirts, caps and brand-related items at events, fairs and promotions.

3. Subscription Programs: Some subscription companies offer a free trial period, allowing customers to try out their services before committing.

4. Birthday Gifts: Loyalty programs can present customers with gifts on their birthdays, showing appreciation for loyalty.

Examples of Successful Companies:

1. Sephora: Sephora is known for offering free samples of beauty products, allowing customers to try different brands before purchasing. This helps build customer loyalty and encourages future purchases.

2. Amazon Prime: Amazon offers a free trial of Amazon Prime, which includes benefits like fast shipping and access to streaming services. This attracts new customers and encourages them to become paying subscribers.

3. Starbucks: Starbucks' rewards program offers gifts like free drinks on customers' birthdays, encouraging loyalty and regular visits.

These examples illustrate how strategically distributing giveaways and free samples can attract customers, build brand loyalty, and drive business growth. However, it's important to ensure that giveaways and samples are on-brand and meet the needs and interests of the target audience.

# 4. Building lasting relationships.

Building Lasting Relationships with the Principle of Reciprocity:

Building lasting relationships based on the principle of reciprocity is fundamental for both professional partnerships and personal friendships. These relationships are characterized by the ongoing exchange of support, trust, and mutual value. Here are some tips on how to build and nurture these relationships over time:

1. Start with Generosity: Start the relationship by being generous. Offer help, share valuable information and be willing to contribute without immediate expectations in return.

2. Be Authentic: Be yourself and show authenticity in your interactions. Authenticity creates deeper, more genuine connections.

3. Communicate Regularly: Maintain regular communication, even if it's just to check up on the

other person. A simple gesture of attention can strengthen a relationship.

4. Listen Carefully: Be willing to listen carefully to others. Show genuine interest in their stories, concerns, and achievements.

5. Offer Support in Times of Need: Be there when others need support. Be empathetic and offer practical help if possible.

6. Keep your Promises: Keep your promises and commitments. This builds trust and credibility over time.

7. Recognize and Appreciate: Recognize the other person's efforts and contributions. Giving thanks and showing appreciation are powerful ways to nurture a relationship.

8. Show Interest in Your Goals: Be interested in the other person's goals and aspirations. Offer your support to help her achieve them.

9. Be Willing to Give In: In conflict situations, be willing to give in and find solutions that benefit both parties. This demonstrates maturity and commitment to the relationship.

10. Grow Together: Seek opportunities to grow and learn together. Participate in joint projects, courses or experiences that strengthen the relationship.

11. Be Patient: Long-lasting relationships can take time to fully develop. Be patient and be willing to invest in building the relationship over time.

12. Maintain Consistency: Consistency in interactions is essential to maintaining lasting relationships. Stay connected even when life is busy.

Reciprocity as a Basis for Partnerships and Friendships:

Reciprocity is the glue that holds lasting relationships together. When both parties are willing to give and receive in a balanced way, the relationship thrives. This applies to both professional partnerships and personal friendships.

In professional partnerships, reciprocity can lead to successful collaborations, resource sharing, and joint growth. In personal friendships, reciprocity creates deep bonds of trust and mutual support.

Remember that reciprocity should not be seen as a commercial transaction, but as an act of generosity and consideration. When both sides are willing to give without expecting something in return immediately, relationships naturally grow stronger over time.

## 5. Success stories with reciprocity.

Success Stories with the Principle of Reciprocity:

1. TOMS Shoes: TOMS is known for its "One for One" model. For every pair of shoes sold, the company donates a pair of shoes to a child in need. This initiative exemplifies reciprocity, as the company gives before receiving. This has resulted in strong support from customers who feel good about purchasing TOMS products, knowing they are contributing to a worthy cause. Additionally, the company expanded its business model to donate sunglasses and eye health services.

2. LinkedIn: The LinkedIn platform is an example of success in applying reciprocity in the digital environment. The company offers a variety of free resources, such as the ability to connect with professionals and access relevant information.

Users are encouraged to share their knowledge and experience through posts and articles. This approach generates engagement and loyalty from users, who are willing to invest time and money in premium features like LinkedIn Premium and LinkedIn Learning.

3. Dropbox: Dropbox, a cloud storage service, has adopted a smart strategy to encourage reciprocity. The company offered free additional storage space to users who recommended the service to friends. This led to rapid growth in the user base as people were willing to share the service in exchange for additional benefits.

4. Ben & Jerry's: The ice cream company Ben & Jerry's is known for its commitment to social responsibility. Not only do they produce delicious ice cream, but they also support social and environmental causes. One of Ben & Jerry's reciprocity strategies is to host "Free Cone Day" annually, during which they offer free ice cream to all customers as a thank you for their continued support. This action creates a strong sense of community and brand loyalty.

5. Non-Profit Organizations: Many non-profit organizations rely heavily on the principle of

reciprocity to raise funds. They organize fundraising events, offer public recognition to donors, and show the direct impact of donations. This approach creates an emotional connection with donors, encouraging them to contribute regularly.

These success stories illustrate how reciprocity can be applied in different sectors and contexts, generating benefits for both companies and communities or customers. The principle of giving before receiving creates meaningful relationships, builds customer loyalty and promotes important causes. It demonstrates that reciprocity is a powerful strategy that goes beyond profit, shaping the way companies and organizations interact with the world around them.

# Chapter 5: Curiosity and FOMO (Fear of Missing Out)



The Role of Curiosity in Mental Triggers:

Curiosity plays a fundamental role in mental triggers, influencing decision-making and human behavior. It can be seen as an intrinsic motivation that drives us to learn, explore and discover. Here is how curiosity plays this role:

1. Intrinsic Motivation: Curiosity is a form of intrinsic motivation, which means it is a motivation that comes from within, not from external rewards. When we're curious about something, we feel compelled to investigate and find out more, regardless of any tangible reward.

2. Stimulating Learning: Curiosity is one of the drivers of learning. When we are curious, we are more willing to seek information, explore new topics, and assimilate knowledge. This is especially relevant in educational and personal development contexts.

3. Decision Making: Curiosity can influence our decisions. For example, when making a choice between products or services, curiosity about the features or benefits offered by each option can affect our final decision.

4. Exploration of New Territories: Curiosity drives us to explore the unknown. This is essential in discovering new opportunities, developing innovations and solving complex problems.

5. Engagement and Entertainment: Curiosity is also fundamental to entertainment and engagement. Intriguing stories, riddles and challenges spark our curiosity and keep us engaged.

Awakening and Using Curiosity Strategically:

Curiosity can be aroused and used strategically in several situations:

1. Captivating Narratives: Telling stories that involve mysteries, unexpected twists or unanswered questions is an effective way to arouse the audience's curiosity.

2.   Thought-provoking   Questions:   Asking open-ended questions that encourage people to think and seek answers is a direct way to spark curiosity.

3. Interactive Experiences: Creating interactive experiences, such as games, challenges or experiments, that require exploration and discovery can stimulate curiosity.

4. Incomplete Information: Presenting incomplete or puzzling information can make people curious and eager for more details.

5. Problem Solving: Challenges that require problem solving and creative thinking often spark curiosity as people want to find an answer.

Curiosity is a powerful motivating force that can positively influence human behavior. Understanding its role in mental triggers and learning to use it strategically can be valuable in a variety of contexts, from marketing to education and personal development. The ability to spark curiosity in people can lead to greater engagement, deeper learning and more informed decision-making.

## 2. Creating FOMO triggers in marketing.

Creating FOMO (Fear of Missing Out) Triggers in Marketing:

"Fear of Missing Out" (FOMO) is a powerful marketing tool that taps into the anxiety people feel when they think they are missing out on something important. This feeling of exclusion can be used effectively in marketing campaigns to drive engagement, conversions, and sales. Here are effective strategies for creating FOMO triggers:

### 1. Exclusivity:

- Early Access: Offer early access to exclusive products, services or content for a select group of customers. This makes them feel privileged and encourages others to want the same special treatment.

- Restricted Invitations: Use invitations or restricted access, where interested parties need to be invited to participate. This creates a sense of belonging to an exclusive group.

- Membership Programs: Create membership programs or VIP clubs with exclusive benefits such as special discounts, premium content or booked events.

2. Scarcity:

- Limited Stock: State that stock is limited, suggesting that the offer may end soon. Phrases like "Only X units available" increase the feeling of scarcity.

- Limited Time Offers: Highlight that a promotion or offer is valid for a short period. This puts pressure on customers to act quickly before the opportunity disappears.

- Countdown: Use countdowns to show how much time is left to take advantage of an exclusive offer or event. This creates a sense of urgency.

3. Social Prova:

- Testimonials and Reviews: Show positive testimonials and reviews from customers who took advantage of the opportunity. This validates other people's decision to participate.

- Social Media Sharing: Encourage customers to share their experiences on social media, creating a sense of belonging to the community and showing that they are enjoying it.

- Mass Participation: Highlight the number of people who have already joined the offer or event. This creates subtle social pressure for others to participate as well.

4. Limited Deadlines:

- Daily Deals: Feature daily or flash deals that change regularly, encouraging customers to come back to check out what's new.

- Flash Discounts: Offer flash discounts or promotions that last just a few hours, encouraging customers to act immediately.

- Unique Events: Announce unique events, such as launches, seasonal sales or exclusive webinars, which only take place on specific dates.

When creating FOMO triggers, it's important to be transparent and authentic. Don't go overboard with scarcity or exclusivity tactics as this can harm customer trust. The goal is to create a legitimate sense of opportunity and excitement, encouraging customers to take action, but without resorting to deceptive tactics. When used ethically, FOMO can be a powerful tool for driving the success of marketing campaigns.

## 3. Teaser and pre-launch strategies.

Teaser and Pre-Launch Strategies:

Teasers and pre-launches are powerful strategies for increasing public curiosity and generating anticipation around products, events or launches. They create a sense of mystery and anticipation that can be highly effective in marketing. Here are some strategies and tips for using teasers and pre-releases effectively:

1. Countdown:

- Create a countdown to a product launch, event, or availability date. This creates a sense of urgency and anticipation.

2. Cryptic Tips:

- Divulge hints or cryptic clues about what's to come. This makes the audience curious and encourages them to try and guess what will be revealed.

3. Teaser Images and Videos:

- Share images or videos that only show a part of the product or event. Don't reveal everything at once; instead, hint at what's to come.

4. Question and Answer Sessions (Q&A):

- Host live Q&A sessions on social media or your website where attendees can ask questions about the launch. Respond with intriguing information, but keep secrets for the big day.

5. "Behind-the-Scenes":

- Show the creation or preparation process behind the launch. This gives the audience an exclusive view and creates empathy with the brand.

6. Stories and Narratives:

- Create an engaging narrative leading up to the launch. Tell a story that increases audience interest and identification.

7. Exclusivity for Subscribers:

- Offer exclusive access to information or products to people who sign up for your email list or follow your social media. This encourages audiences to engage more with your brand.

Examples of Companies:

1. Apple: Apple is known for its highly secretive pre-launch campaigns and intriguing teasers before new product launches like iPhones and iPads. They reveal details in stages, keeping the audience in suspense.

2. Marvel Studios: Marvel generates great anticipation around its superhero films through teasers and trailers that offer just glimpses of the stories and characters.

3. Tesla: Tesla uses teasers and pre-launches to generate interest in its new electric vehicles. They

reveal information gradually, keeping enthusiasts engaged and curious.

Tips for Creating Effective Teasers:

- Maintain a balance between revealing enough to create interest and maintaining the audience's curiosity.
- Use suggestive language and images that leave room for interpretation.
- Maintain consistency with your brand identity and the message you want to convey.
- Leverage social media and content marketing to amplify your teasers.
- Interact with your audience on social media, responding to questions and comments to maintain engagement.

Remember, the main purpose of teasers and pre-releases is to create an engaging experience for your audience and generate genuine excitement around what's coming up. The more intriguing and well-executed they are, the more impact they will have on your marketing strategy.

# 4. How to maintain the public's interest.

How to Keep the Audience Interested:

Maintaining your audience's interest is just as important as sparking it initially, especially when it comes to building lasting relationships and maximizing the value of your marketing efforts. Here are some considerations on the importance of maintaining interest and strategies for doing so:

1. Importance of Maintaining Interest:

- Building Lasting Relationships: Maintaining the public's interest is essential to building lasting relationships. This builds brand loyalty and can lead to repeat sales or continued support.

- Value Maximization: By maintaining the audience's interest, you can extract more value from each customer or follower. Satisfied customers are more likely to purchase again or invest in additional products or services.

- Advocacy Generation: People who remain interested in your brand or content are more likely to become advocates and promoters, sharing their experiences with others.

2. Strategies to Maintain Interest:

- Consistent Delivery of Value: Continue to offer content, products or services that add value to your audience's lives. Make sure your offerings meet your audience's evolving needs.

- Continuous Communication: Maintain regular and relevant communication with your audience through newsletters, social networks, blogs or other platforms. Be present and engaging.

- Personalization: Use data and analytics to personalize the customer experience. This could include personalized recommendations, special offers, or targeted content.

- Feedback and Involvement: Ask for feedback and involve your audience in important decisions. It makes them feel like they have a voice and influence on your brand.

- High-Quality Content: Continue to create high-quality content that is informative, engaging, and relevant to your audience. Stay up to date with trends in your industry.

- Loyalty Programs: Create loyalty programs that reward loyal customers. This encourages repeat business.

- Events and Communities: Organize events, webinars or create online communities where your audience can gather, share experiences and learn more.

3. Surprise and Innovate: Keep the public's interest by surprising them from time to time. This may involve launching new products, services or innovative initiatives that make a positive impact.

4. Continuous Learning: Be willing to learn from your audience. Understand your changing needs and wants and adapt your strategies accordingly.

5. Crisis Management: In crisis or problem situations, deal with them transparently and effectively. This can demonstrate responsibility and concern for the public.

6. Coherence in Message and Values: Maintain consistency in your message and values over time. This strengthens your brand identity and public trust.

7. Ongoing Feedback: Be open to ongoing feedback from the public and make improvements based on that feedback. This shows that you value their opinions.

8. Early Access and Exclusivity: Continue to offer early access and exclusivity to products or content to reward audience loyalty.

Remember that maintaining the public's interest is a constant effort that requires dedication and care. The audience changes over time, and your strategies need to adapt to these changes. The key is to build a relationship of trust and mutual value that benefits both your brand and your audience.

## 5. Case studies using curiosity.

Case Studies Using Curiosity:

1. Airbnb - "The Night at the Museum": Airbnb launched a campaign in partnership with the Louvre Museum in Paris, offering a unique night to one lucky winner: the opportunity to sleep in the museum. The concept explored many people's curiosity about what happens behind the scenes of the famous museum at night. The winner had the chance to spend the night in a special space, surrounded by masterpieces and had a unique experience. This campaign generated a lot of buzz on social media, highlighting how curiosity can be used to engage audiences.

2. Mystery Science Theater 3000 - Kickstarter: The cult series "Mystery Science Theater 3000" raised more than $6 million in a crowdfunding campaign on Kickstarter to create new episodes. The series is known for its unique premise of people watching bad movies and making sarcastic comments during the viewing. The campaign tapped into fans' curiosity about what would happen if the series came back to life, and offered intriguing rewards like participating in live episodes. This demonstrates how curiosity can drive crowdfunding and reignite interest in an intellectual property.

3. Burger King - "The Whopper in White": Burger King launched a campaign where it asked its

customers to trust the brand and order a "Whopper in white", that is, without knowing what was in the burger. This campaign appealed to people's curiosity and the idea that they were about to discover something new and unique. The campaign was a hit on social media, highlighting how curiosity can be used to engage audiences in a brand experience.

4. National Geographic - "Genius": National Geographic launched a series called "Genius", which explored the lives of historical figures such as Albert Einstein and Pablo Picasso. The marketing campaign tapped into people's curiosity about the lives and minds of these iconic personalities. They released intriguing teasers and shared behind-the-scenes content to keep the audience curious and engaged. This exemplifies how curiosity can be used to promote TV shows and educational content.

5. The New York Times - "The Truth Is Worth It": This marketing campaign from The New York Times highlighted the importance of quality journalism and tapped into people's curiosity about how news is investigated and reported. The series of ads showcased the reporting process and the challenges journalists face in uncovering the truth.

The campaign emphasized that "the truth is worth it" and received recognition for its engaging and informative approach.

These case studies illustrate how curiosity can be a powerful tool in marketing campaigns and creative projects. By tapping into the natural human desire to discover, these campaigns have managed to engage audiences and generate genuine interest. Curiosity can be applied effectively in a variety of contexts and industries, from tourism to journalism and entertainment.

# Chapter 6: Emotions and Human Connection

# 1. The influence of emotions on mental triggers.

The Influence of Emotions on Mental Triggers:

Emotions play a fundamental role in mental triggers and human behavior. They are powerful drivers of decisions and actions, and companies often use emotional strategies to influence consumers' perceptions and choices. Here is a deeper exploration of this topic:

## 1. The Emotional Nature of Decision Making:

- Many human decisions are made based on emotions, not just logic. Emotions influence our judgments, preferences and actions in significant ways.

- The psychology behind this is partly due to the fact that emotions provide a quick way to evaluate information and make decisions. In risky situations, for example, anxiety or fear can signal danger and motivate quick actions.

2. Emotion-Based Mental Triggers:

- Various mental triggers exploit emotions to influence behavior. Some examples include scarcity (creates anxiety about missing out), reciprocity (generates feelings of gratitude), and authority (inspires trust).

- Curiosity, mentioned previously, is also a mental trigger that works through emotion. The feeling of wanting to discover something new and intriguing is driven by curiosity.

3. Examples of Using Emotions in Marketing:

- Coca-Cola - Christmas Campaign: Coca-Cola is known for its emotional Christmas campaigns. Your ads often depict moments of family togetherness and friendship, creating an emotional association with your brand.

- Nike - "Just Do It": Nike often uses motivational and emotional messages in its advertising. The phrase "Just Do It" evokes feelings of courage and determination, associating these emotions with its products.

- Charity Campaigns - Exploring Empathy: Charitable organizations often appeal to the public's emotions by showing images of people in difficult situations. This generates empathy and motivates people to contribute to noble causes.

- Car Commercials - Euphoria and Freedom: Many car advertisements emphasize the thrill of driving and the feeling of freedom it brings. This creates an emotional attachment to the idea of owning a particular vehicle.

4. Emotion Management in Marketing:

- Companies need to be sensitive to the use of emotions in their campaigns, as they can affect both positively and negatively the public's perception.

- Emotion management involves understanding consumers' emotions, recognizing emotions associated with the brand, and ensuring that messages and actions are aligned with the desired emotional image.

- It is important to remember that the emotions evoked must be authentic and relevant to the brand

and product, as inappropriate use of emotions can damage credibility.

Emotions play a central role in mental triggers and marketing. By understanding how emotions influence human behavior and using emotional strategies ethically and authentically, companies can create deeper connections with their audiences and positively influence consumer perceptions and choices.

## 2. Identifying your target audience's emotions.

Identifying Your Target Audience's Emotions:

Understanding the predominant emotions of your target audience is key to creating effective marketing and communication strategies. Here are some guidelines on how to identify these emotions:

1. Market Research:

- Conduct market research to gain insights into your audience's emotions. Open-ended questions that ask participants to describe how they feel about your product or service can reveal underlying emotions.

- Use customer satisfaction and feedback surveys to identify the emotions associated with their experience with your brand. Analyze comments and emotional responses.

2. Social Media Analysis:

- Monitor social media conversations related to your brand, products or industry. People often share emotions, praise and criticism on social media.

- Use social media analytics tools to identify keywords and hashtags related to specific emotions. This can help you understand how your audience feels about your business.

3. Interviews and In-Depth Interviews:

- Conduct interviews with customers or target audience members to gain a deeper understanding of their emotions. Ask about their experiences, challenges and aspirations and be aware of emotional responses.

- In-depth interviews allow you to delve deeper into emotions, exploring personal stories and narratives that reveal feelings.

4. Behavioral Data Analysis:

- Analyze customer behavioral data such as purchasing patterns, retention and engagement rates. This data can provide clues about the emotions that motivate your decisions.

- Identify moments of high and low emotion throughout the customer cycle to understand how emotions affect interactions with your brand.


5. Competition Assessment:

- Analyze how your competition communicates and how customers react emotionally to them. This can help you identify opportunities to excel emotionally.

- Observe what emotions your competitors are tapping into and consider whether you want to follow suit or take a different approach.

The Importance of Understanding Specific Emotions:

Understanding the specific emotions that drive purchasing or engagement decisions is vital for several reasons:

1. Personalization: Allows you to personalize your messages and offers according to the emotional needs of your target audience.

2. Emotional Connection: Helps build a deeper emotional connection with customers, which can lead to longer-lasting relationships.

3. Effective Messaging: Allows you to create more effective marketing messages as you can tap into the right emotions that motivate action.

4. Problem Solving: Helps you identify specific problems or challenges your customers are facing, allowing you to adapt your products or services to meet them.

Research and Analysis Methods:

- Use sentiment analysis software to examine online comments and reviews for positive or negative emotions.

- Hold focus groups to hear the opinions and emotions of a group of people at the same time.

- Create surveys that include emotional rating scales to measure the level of emotion associated with certain topics or products.

- Use data analysis tools to identify emotional trends in large data sets.

Remembering that emotions can vary from person to person and from culture to culture, it is important to consider the diversity of your audience when analyzing and using this emotional information in your marketing and communication strategies.


## 3. Narrative and storytelling as emotional tools.

Narrative and Storytelling as Emotional Tools:

Narrative and storytelling are powerful tools for evoking emotions and creating deep emotional connections with the audience. Here are some key points about how they work:

1. Evoking Emotions:

- Stories have the power to convey emotions in a vivid and memorable way. By presenting characters, situations and conflicts, narratives allow the audience to identify with the characters' experiences, awakening emotions such as empathy, joy, sadness, anger, surprise, among others.

2. Emotional Connections:

- Stories can create lasting emotional connections because the audience feels invested in the characters' trajectories and plot twists. This helps build deeper relationships with the brand or message being communicated.

3. Examples of Effective Storytelling in Marketing and Communication:

- Dove - "Real Beauty" Campaign: Dove used stories of real women and their journeys of self-acceptance to promote its line of beauty products. These stories evoked empathy and resonated with audiences, generating an emotional connection and a positive message about real beauty.

- Apple - Christmas Commercials: Apple is known for its emotional Christmas commercials that tell stories of families coming together during the festive season. These commercials evoke emotions of warmth, love and togetherness, associating these feelings with the Apple brand.

- Google - "Loretta": Google's commercial during the 2020 Super Bowl told the story of an elderly man who used Google Assistant to remember his late wife. The story was moving and evoked deep empathy, showing how technology can have a significant emotional impact.

4. Tips for Building Impactful Narratives:

- Identify the Target Audience: Know your target audience and their predominant emotions to adapt your narrative to them.

- Develop Captivating Characters: Create authentic, complex characters that audiences can identify with.

- Conflict and Resolution: Every good story has a conflict and a resolution. This keeps the audience engaged.

- Be Authentic: Tell authentic stories that relate to your brand's values and mission.

- Use Visual and Auditory Elements: Visual and auditory elements, such as images, music and voice, can amplify emotion in a narrative.

- Simplicity: Keep the narrative simple and focused. Avoid distractions that can dilute the emotion.

- Take Adequate Time: Don't be in a rush to tell your story. Allow the audience to become involved with the characters and plot.

- Call to Action: At the end of the story, provide a call to action that capitalizes on the emotion generated by the narrative.

Narrative and storytelling are powerful tools for evoking emotions and creating emotional connections with the audience. By telling authentic, captivating stories that resonate with your audience's values and aspirations, you can engage them more deeply and effectively.

4. Successful emotional advertising campaigns.

Successful Emotional Advertising Campaigns:

1. Nike - "Dream Crazy" (2018): This commercial featured Colin Kaepernick and other athletes, celebrating the fight for social justice and the pursuit of dreams. The campaign evoked emotions of courage and determination in addressing important social issues. Result: Nike saw increased sales and a wave of support on social media, despite facing some controversy.

2. Google - "Dear Sophie" (2011): This heartwarming Google commercial showed a father creating an email account for his daughter from birth through childhood. The story evoked feelings of nostalgia and love. Result: The commercial was highly praised for its emotionality and contributed to a positive image of the Google brand.

3. Always - "Like a Girl" (2014): This campaign challenged gender stereotypes by asking people to do activities "like a girl." The message was empowering and inspiring, promoting girls' self-esteem. Result: The campaign went viral and raised awareness about gender issues, generating a positive response on social media.

4. Coca-Cola - "Hilltop" (1971): This iconic commercial featured people from all over the world singing "I'd Like to Buy the World a Coke." The message was one of peace and global unity. Result: The campaign was a success and became one of the most famous advertisements in history, solidifying Coca-Cola as a brand associated with happiness and harmony.

5. Budweiser - "Puppy Love" (2014): This Super Bowl ad showed the friendship between a puppy and a Clydesdale horse. The story touched audiences with emotions of love and connection. Result: The commercial was widely praised and helped Budweiser gain significant exposure during the Super Bowl.

6. Dove - "Real Beauty Sketches" (2013): Dove launched a social experiment in which women described themselves to a portrait artist and then

had someone else describe them. The campaign highlighted women's self-image and evoked emotions of self-esteem and acceptance. Result: The video went viral and sparked conversations about real beauty, resulting in a positive image for the Dove brand.

These advertising campaigns are notable examples of how the effective use of emotions can generate impact and engagement with the public. They addressed relevant topics, told authentic stories and evoked an authentic emotional response, which resulted in recognition, support on social media and, in many cases, increased sales and brand image.

## 5. Building genuine connections with customers.

Building Genuine Customer Connections:

Building genuine connections with customers through understanding and utilizing emotions is essential to the long-term success of any business. Here are strategies and examples for establishing lasting, loyal relationships based on emotional connection:

1. Actively Listen:

- Demonstrate genuine interest in understanding your customers' concerns, needs and desires. This can be done through surveys, direct feedback and social media monitoring.

Example: Zappos, an online shoe retailer, is known for its exceptional customer service, which starts with the practice of active listening. They strive to understand customers' emotions and needs in every interaction.

2. Empathy Exhibitions:

- Put yourself in the customer's shoes and understand their emotional perspectives. Respond with empathy when customers face challenges or frustrations.

Example: Southwest Airlines is often praised for its empathy in difficult situations, such as accommodating passengers affected by flight delays or cancellations, demonstrating genuine care.

3. Tell Authentic Stories:

- Share stories that showcase the mission, values and people behind your brand. Authentic stories evoke emotions and connect customers to your company.

Example: TOMS, known for its "One for One" philosophy, shares stories of people who have benefited from its shoe donations, creating an emotional connection with consumers.

4. Personalize Interactions:

- Use data to personalize customer interactions. Show that you know them, understand their preferences, and are willing to accommodate their individual needs.

Example: Amazon is a master at personalization, recommending products based on a customer's purchasing history and browsing behavior, creating a highly relevant and emotional experience.

5. Recognize and Thank:

- Recognize and thank customers for their loyalty. Small gestures, like personalized thank you notes, can create strong emotional bonds.

Example: Starbucks has a loyalty program that rewards customers with free drinks and other benefits, showing gratitude for their coffee choice.

6. Communicate Shared Values:

- Clearly communicate your company values and how they align with customer values. This creates an emotional connection based on shared values.

Example: Patagonia, an outdoor clothing brand, is known for its environmental advocacy and communicates its environmental values to attract consumers who share this concern.

7. Take Responsibility:

- If you make mistakes, take responsibility and do your best to correct them. Honesty and a willingness to fix problems can create a stronger emotional connection.

Example: Johnson & Johnson dealt with a public relations crisis in 1982 when some of its products were contaminated. The company took full responsibility and recalled all affected products, rebuilding consumer trust.

Building genuine connections with customers is not just about business transactions, but about building relationships based on trust, empathy and authenticity. Companies that adopt these strategies can cultivate a loyal customer base that not only purchases repeatedly but also advocates and promotes the brand.

# Chapter 7: Social Proof and Herd Behavior

How Social Proof Affects Purchasing Decisions:

Social proof is one of the most influential psychological principles affecting people's purchasing decisions. It is based on the idea that when people are uncertain about what action to take, they tend to look to others for guidance. Here are details on how social proof influences purchasing decisions:

1. Trust in the Experience of Others:

- People naturally trust the experiences and opinions of others, such as friends, family, colleagues and even strangers, to make informed decisions about products or services.

Example: When someone is thinking about buying a new cell phone, it is common to ask friends who already have the same model about their experience and satisfaction.

2. Social Validation:

- People seek social validation, which means they want to make decisions that are socially acceptable and approved. This leads them to follow the behavior of others as a guide to action.

Example: In a crowded restaurant, people often choose dishes that are popular or recommended by other customers, assuming that these dishes are of high quality.

3. Risk Reduction:

- Social proof reduces the perceived risk of making a bad decision. If many other people have had positive experiences, someone is more likely to feel safe following the same path.

Example: Product and service reviews on sites like Amazon and TripAdvisor provide buyers with valuable information from other consumers to make more informed decisions.

4. Social Media Influence:

- Social media has amplified social proof as people can now share their experiences and opinions on a global scale. Reviews, comments and shares on social media have a huge impact on purchasing decisions.

Example: Digital influencers often use their platforms to recommend products or services, and followers trust their opinions.

5. Marketing Strategies:

- Companies use social proof in their marketing strategies in a variety of ways, including customer testimonials, product reviews, social media follower counts, and awards or certifications.

Example: An e-commerce site can display customer reviews alongside products to provide social evidence of product quality.

6. Bandwagon Effect:

- The "bandwagon" effect occurs when people follow the crowd, assuming something is good or right simply because so many others are doing it. This is a direct manifestation of social proof.

Example: During a sale, people may buy items just because others are buying them, creating a herd effect.

In short, social proof plays a key role in purchasing decisions as people rely on the experiences and opinions of others to guide their choices. Understanding this phenomenon is essential for companies that want to positively influence consumer behavior and build trust in their products and services.

## 2. Customer testimonials and reviews.

Customer Testimonials and Reviews as Effective Forms of Social Proof:

Customer testimonials and reviews are highly effective social proof tools as they offer real evidence of customer satisfaction and the quality of a product or service. Here's how they work and how to use them effectively:

1. Tangible Evidence:

- Testimonials and reviews provide tangible evidence of other customers' experience with your product or service. They show that real people have had positive results.

2. Building Trust:

- When potential customers see positive testimonials and reviews, it builds trust as they feel more confident about their purchasing decision.

3. Reduction of Uncertainty:

- Reviews and testimonials help reduce the uncertainty buyers may feel when considering an unfamiliar product or service. This is especially important when shopping online.

4. Decision-Making Support:

- Reviews and testimonials can help buyers make more informed decisions by allowing them to consider the experience of others before making a choice.

Guidelines for Collecting and Using Testimonials in a Convincing Way:

1. Ask for Feedback:

- Request feedback from satisfied customers and encourage them to share their experiences. Ask specifically about aspects you want to highlight, such as quality, customer service, or ease of use.

2. Be Authentic:

- Use genuine and real testimonials. Avoid creating or editing testimonials to make them look better than they are, as authenticity is key.

3. Diversity of Experiences:

- Collect testimonials from customers with different experiences and perspectives. This helps showcase the versatility and breadth of your product or service.

4. Display Visibly:

- Place testimonials in strategic locations on your website, product page or marketing materials where visitors can easily see them.

5. Include Relevant Details:

- Make sure testimonials include specific details about how the product or service helped the customer, which makes the story more compelling.

6. Use Star Ratings:

- If applicable, use star rating systems (e.g. 1 to 5) to summarize customer reviews in a quick and visually appealing way.

7. Respond to Reviews:

- Show that you value customer opinions by responding to reviews, whether positive or negative. This demonstrates transparency and concern for customer satisfaction.

8. Create a Space for Testimonials:

- Consider creating a dedicated section on your website or a third-party review platform for customer testimonials and reviews.

Importance of Authenticity and Transparency:

Maintaining authenticity is essential when using testimonials and reviews. Faking or editing testimonials can erode customer trust and damage your brand reputation. Transparency is also key, especially when dealing with negative reviews. Addressing criticism in a constructive and transparent way can even improve the company's image.

Customer testimonials and reviews are powerful social proof tools that positively influence purchasing decisions. Collecting, displaying and using testimonials in an authentic and transparent way helps build consumer trust and strengthen your brand image.

## 3. Success stories with influencers.

Success Stories with Influencers in Social Proof:

1. Daniel Wellington and Influencers on Instagram:

- The watch brand Daniel Wellington stood out by collaborating with influencers on Instagram. They provided influencers with stylish watches so they could share photos wearing the products. The result was a significant increase in brand visibility and sales.

2. Glossier and Partnerships with Beauty Bloggers:

- Glossier, a cosmetics brand, collaborated with several influential beauty bloggers to review and promote their products. Bloggers shared authentic reviews and makeup tutorials, helping build the brand's credibility as a high-quality, affordable beauty option.

3. Airbnb and Campaign with YouTubers:

- Airbnb launched a campaign in partnership with YouTubers who showcased their unique travel experiences in Airbnb rentals. These videos inspired potential travelers and provided social proof about the quality of accommodations offered.

4. Nike and Featured Athletes:

- Nike has a history of collaborating with prominent athletes such as Michael Jordan and LeBron James. These partnerships not only promote products, but also reinforce the brand's credibility and prestige, associating it with high-level athletes.

How Partnering with Influencers Increases Credibility and Visibility:

- Influencers have a captive audience that trusts their opinions and recommendations. When an influencer shares a positive experience with a product or brand, it serves as social proof for their audience.

- Partnering with influencers can increase brand visibility, reaching a wider audience than traditional marketing methods. This is especially effective when influencers have followers that fit the brand's target audience.

- Influencers can often create authentic and engaging content around a product or service, which resonates better with consumers than traditional advertisements.

Criteria for Choosing Influencers:


1. Relevance:

- The influencer must be relevant to the brand's target audience. The affinity between the influencer and the product is essential for the message to be authentic.

2. Credibility:

- Make sure the influencer is known for providing honest and trustworthy reviews. This increases the credibility of the partnership.

3. Engagement:

- Evaluate the influencer's level of engagement with their audience. An influencer with an active community tends to have a greater impact.

4. Shared Values:

- Make sure the influencer's values and image are aligned with those of the brand. Partnerships with influencers whose values coincide with those of the company tend to be more authentic.

5. History of Successful Collaborations:

- Analyze the influencer's past collaborations with other brands. A history of successful partnerships is a good indication.

6. Target Audience:

– Consider whether the influencer's audience is similar to your target audience. This will help ensure the message reaches the right people.

Influencer partnerships can be a powerful social proof strategy, as long as they are carefully selected and aligned with the brand in an authentic and transparent way. When done correctly, these collaborations can significantly increase brand credibility and visibility.

# 4. Using convincing numbers and statistics.

Using Numbers and Statistics as Solid Social Proof:

Numbers and statistics are powerful forms of social proof, as they provide objective and measurable evidence of the success of a product, service or brand. Here is how they can be used effectively:

## 1. Validating Claims:

- Numbers can validate claims made by a company. For example, a food company may use laboratory test data to prove that its products are healthier compared to the competition.

Example: Streaming company Netflix often uses viewership data to show which shows and movies are the most popular, validating their value to subscribers.

## 2. Demonstrating Growth and Success:

- Statistics can show the growth and success of a company over time. This can be particularly convincing for investors and potential customers.

Example: Apple often highlights sales and revenue numbers in its quarterly financial reports to demonstrate its ongoing performance.

## 3. Comparing to the Competition:

- Numbers and statistics can be used to compare a company's performance with that of its competitors, highlighting competitive advantages.

Example: Coca-Cola often compares its sales and market share to Pepsi to demonstrate its leadership in the beverage industry.

4. Reinforcing Effectiveness:

- Data can show how effective a product or service is in solving specific problems. This helps build trust among consumers.

Example: Pharmaceutical companies often use clinical trials and statistics to demonstrate the effectiveness of medications.

Guidelines for Presenting Data Clearly:

1. Simplify Complexity:

   - Make complex data accessible to the public, using graphs, infographics or visualizations that simplify the information.

2. Highlight Key Points:

- Identify the most important points in the data and highlight them so they are easily understandable.

3. Contextualize the Numbers:

- Provide context for the numbers, explaining what they mean in practical terms for customers or investors.

4. Use Reliable Sources:

- Make sure the data comes from reliable and reputable sources to avoid any questions about its veracity.

5. Be Transparent:

- Be transparent about the methodology used to collect the data and avoid manipulating information to appear more favorable than it is.

Examples of Companies that Used Statistical Data in Marketing Strategies:

1. Google Trends:

- Google Trends offers information about users' search trends. Many companies use this data to adjust their marketing strategies based on what's trending.

2. Amazon:

- Amazon uses product reviews and ratings extensively on its website, providing buyers with quantitative information about a product's quality.

3. Spotify:

- Spotify creates personalized playlists based on statistical data about users' listening habits, demonstrating its ability to offer a tailored music experience.

In short, numbers and statistics are solid forms of social proof that can be used to validate claims, demonstrate success, benchmark against the competition, and reinforce the effectiveness of products or services. By presenting data in a clear and transparent way, companies can build trust and positively influence the perception of consumers and investors.

## 5. Strategies to encourage herd behavior.

Strategies to Encourage Herd Behavior:

Herd behavior refers to the tendency of people to follow the actions, opinions, and decisions of a group, often in response to a desire for belonging and social conformity. Encouraging this behavior among consumers can be an effective marketing strategy. Here are some practical strategies:

1. Creating a Sense of Belonging:

- Online Community: Create an online community around your brand or product. This can be done through forums, social media groups or dedicated platforms. Community members will feel part of something bigger.

Example: Apple has a community of enthusiastic users who gather in online forums to discuss products, troubleshoot problems, and share tips.

- Loyalty Programs: Develop loyalty programs that reward customers for frequent purchases. They will feel like they are part of an exclusive club and will be encouraged to keep shopping.

Example: Starbucks Rewards offers rewards and access to exclusive offers for frequent members.

2. User Generated Content:

- Encourage customers to create content related to your brand or product. This could be reviews, photos, videos or stories. User-generated content helps you build an authentic narrative around your product.

Example: GoPro is known for sharing amazing videos created by its customers, encouraging others to do the same.

3. Challenges and Viral Campaigns:

- Create challenges or campaigns that encourage consumers to participate and challenge their friends to do the same. These campaigns can spread quickly on social media.

Example: The "Ice Bucket Challenge" was a viral campaign that raised funds for amyotrophic lateral sclerosis (ALS) research and encouraged many people to participate.

4. Exclusivity and Limited Edition:

- Offer exclusive, limited edition products or experiences. This creates a sense of urgency and makes people want to be part of this select group.

Example: Supreme, a streetwear brand, is known for releasing limited edition products that quickly sell out, creating a strong sense of exclusivity.

5. Events and Activations:

- Hold in-person or virtual events that bring your customers together. These shared experiences strengthen the feeling of belonging.

Example: Nike organizes races in cities around the world, such as the "Nike Run Club," which brings together runners and creates a sense of community.

6. Referral Discount:

- Offer discounts or rewards to customers who refer friends to your brand or service. This encourages word-of-mouth sharing.

Example: Dropbox offered extra storage space to users who referred friends, encouraging user base growth.

Remember that authenticity is key when using these strategies. Consumers may detect artificial attempts to encourage herding behavior. Therefore, it is important to build a genuine community and provide value to members so that they want to be part of it and share their experiences with others.

# Chapter 8: Implementation and Measurement of Results

## 1. Incorporating mental triggers into your strategy.

Incorporating Mental Triggers into Your Marketing Strategy:

Incorporating mental triggers into your marketing strategy is essential because they are powerful psychological influence tools that can impact the decisions and actions of your target audience. Here is the importance of doing so and how you can do it effectively:

Importance of Incorporating Mental Triggers:

1. Increases Persuasion: Mental triggers have the power to persuade people to take certain actions, such as purchasing a product, signing up for a newsletter, or sharing content. They activate human instincts and influence decision-making.

2. Creates Emotional Connection: By incorporating mental triggers, you can create a deeper emotional connection with your audience. This helps build brand loyalty and build lasting relationships.

3. Stand Out from the Competition: Strategies that use mental triggers effectively can stand out in a crowded market because they can attract attention and resonate with the audience's needs and desires in a unique way.

Guidelines for Incorporating Mental Triggers:

1. Understand Your Target Audience:

   - Before incorporating mental triggers, it is crucial to understand who your target audience is. Market research, data analysis, and segmentation will help you identify your audience's needs, wants, and motivations.

2. Identify Relevant Triggers:

   - Once you understand your target audience, identify the mental triggers most relevant to them. Some common triggers include scarcity, urgency, reciprocity, authority, and social proof. Choose the ones that best align with your goals.

3. Align with Brand Message:

   - Make sure the mental triggers you choose align with the overall message of your brand or campaign. They should complement and reinforce the narrative you are building.

4. Be Authentic:

- Avoid excessive or manipulative use of mental triggers. Authenticity is key to building trust with your audience. Use triggers ethically and honestly.

5. Test and Measure Results:

- Apply mental triggers to your strategy and monitor the results. Test different approaches and messages to see which works best with your audience.

Example of Mental Trigger Incorporation:

Imagine you are marketing an online course on productivity. After researching your target audience, you've identified that they value saving time and want to increase their efficiency at work. Here are some ways to incorporate mental triggers:

- Scarcity and Urgency: Offer the course for a limited time with a special discount for first-time enrollees, creating a sense of urgency.

- Social Proof: Share testimonials from previous students who increased their productivity after taking the course.

- Authority: Highlight your own track record of success in the area of productivity to show your authority on the subject.

By incorporating these mental triggers, you are aligning your strategy with your audience's wants and needs, increasing the persuasiveness and effectiveness of your marketing message.

## 2. Tools and resources for creating mental triggers.

Tools and Resources for Creating Mental Triggers:

1. Market Research and Data Analysis:
    - Google Trends: Allows you to monitor search trends.
    - Google Analytics: Provides detailed information about user behavior on your website.

- SurveyMonkey: Helps collect feedback and survey data.

2. Content Marketing:
- Blogs and Social Networks: Platforms such as WordPress, Blogger, Facebook, Instagram and Twitter are excellent for sharing content that incorporates mental triggers.
- Content Scheduling Tools: Hootsuite and Buffer can help schedule posts to optimize when mental triggers are activated.

3. E-mail Marketing:
- MailChimp: Allows you to create effective email marketing campaigns with scarcity, urgency and personalization triggers.
- ConvertKit: Specialized in email marketing automation to create personalized mental triggers.

4. Testing and Optimization:
- Google Optimize: Helps you perform A/B tests to optimize the effectiveness of mental triggers on your website.
- Hotjar: Offers user behavior analysis to identify where mental triggers are most effective.

5. Graphic Design and Multimedia:

- Adobe Creative Cloud: Offers a full suite of design tools, including Photoshop and Illustrator, to create compelling images and videos that embody mental triggers.

6. Marketing Automation:
- HubSpot: Enables marketing automation to personalize messages based on user behavior, including mental triggers.
- Marketo: Offers advanced marketing automation solutions that can incorporate mental triggers into campaigns.

7. Courses and Books:
- "Influence: The Psychology of Persuasion" by Robert Cialdini: A classic book that explores the principles of persuasion, including mental triggers.
- Online Courses: Platforms such as Coursera, Udemy and edX offer courses on consumer psychology, persuasion and marketing that can deepen your knowledge about mental triggers.

8. Project Management Software:
- Trello: Helps organize and manage marketing projects that incorporate mental triggers.
- Asana: Makes it easier to track tasks and deadlines to implement mental trigger strategies.

9. Social Networks and Online Ads:

- Facebook Ads Manager: Allows advanced targeting based on demographic, behavioral and interest data, ideal for social proof and authority triggers.

- LinkedIn Ads: Great for B2B marketing, using mental triggers related to authority and trust.

10. Data Analysis and Metrics:

- Google Data Studio: Create custom dashboards to track key metrics related to mental triggers.

- HubSpot Analytics: Delivers advanced insights into the performance of your mental trigger strategies.

11. E-commerce Platforms:

- Shopify: An ecommerce platform with features to implement scarcity, urgency and personalization triggers on your product pages.

Choosing the right tools depends on the specific goals of your marketing strategy and target audience. By selecting the right platforms and technologies, you can facilitate the effective implementation of mental triggers and improve the performance of your campaigns.

### 3. Testing and optimizing mental triggers.

Testing and Optimizing Mental Triggers in a Strategy:

Testing and optimizing mental triggers in your marketing strategy is crucial to maximizing effectiveness and achieving the best results possible. Here's why it matters and how to do it:

Importance of Testing and Optimizing Mental Triggers:

1. Improves Conversion: Testing different mental triggers allows you to discover which are most effective in convincing your audience to take the desired action, whether buying a product, subscribing to a newsletter or sharing content.

2. Adjusts to the Target Audience: Each audience is unique, and what works for one may not work for another. Testing helps you adapt your mental triggers to your audience's specific preferences and behaviors.

3. Increases Return on Investment (ROI): By optimizing your strategies based on test results, you spend your marketing budget more efficiently, increasing ROI.

Testing and Analysis Methods:

1. A/B tests:

   - Perform A/B tests on your campaigns. This involves creating two versions of the same campaign, one with a specific mental trigger and one with a different one. The version that generates best results is chosen.

2. Multivariable Test:

   - Go beyond A/B testing and test multiple elements of your campaigns at the same time, including different mental triggers. This helps you understand how different combinations of elements affect audience response.

3. Data Analysis:

   - Use data analytics tools like Google Analytics to track user behavior and conversions related to specific mental triggers. Identify which triggers perform best.

4. Qualitative and Quantitative Research:

- Conduct qualitative and quantitative research to get direct feedback from customers on how mental triggers affect their decisions. This may include interviews, online surveys and focus groups.

5. Audience Segmentation:

   - Segmenting your audience allows you to test different mental triggers in specific groups. For example, you can test a trigger based on your audience's age or interests to see which is most effective in each segment.

Iteration and Continuous Improvement:

- Optimization is not a single process; it is continuous. As you collect data and test results, use this information to iterate and improve your mental trigger strategies. This may involve adjusting messages, images, mental trigger positions, and even choosing different triggers based on ongoing learning.

- Be willing to adapt your strategies based on changes in your target audience's preferences and behaviors. As the effectiveness of a mental trigger decreases over time, it may be necessary to test new approaches.

- Keep records of all tests and results to track trends over time. This will help you build a solid understanding of how mental triggers affect your audience and how you can continually improve your strategies.

Remember, the key to success is being adaptable and committed to finding the approaches that work best for your specific audience. Testing and optimizing mental triggers is a valuable process for improving your marketing strategy and increasing your ability to influence consumer behavior.

## 4. Performance evaluation and relevant metrics.

Performance Assessment and Relevant Metrics for Mental Triggers:

Evaluating the performance of mental triggers is essential for measuring the impact of your marketing and persuasion strategies. Here are some relevant metrics and performance indicators, including how to evaluate ROI:

1. Conversion Rate:
   - This is a fundamental metric that measures the percentage of visitors who took the desired action, such as purchasing a product, filling out a form, or signing up for a newsletter. It indicates how effective your mental triggers are in persuading your audience.

2. Taxa de Cliques (CTR - Click-Through Rate):
   - Measures the proportion of people who clicked on a specific element, such as a buy button or a link, relative to the total number of people who saw the element. A high CTR may indicate that your mental triggers are encouraging action.

3. Time Spent on Page:
   - Assessing how long visitors spend on a page after being exposed to mental triggers can indicate the level of engagement generated by those triggers. The longer people stay, the greater the impact.

4. Bounce Rate:
   - This metric tells you how many visitors leave immediately after landing on your page. A low

rejection rate suggests that mental triggers are keeping people engaged and interested.

## 5. Return on Investment (ROI):

- Assessing ROI is crucial to determine whether your mental triggers are generating positive results in relation to the costs involved. Calculate ROI by comparing the value of conversions (e.g. revenue generated) with the costs of implementing the strategy.

## 6. Email Open Rate:

- For email marketing campaigns, this metric indicates how many people opened your emails. If your emails include mental triggers to encourage opens, this metric is relevant.

## 7. Email Click Rate:

- In addition to the open rate, this metric measures how many people clicked on the links or buttons within the emails. This is particularly relevant when you use mental triggers in your messages.

## 8. Email Conversion Rate:

- This metric measures the percentage of email recipients who completed the desired action, such as making a purchase, after receiving your email. It can be used to evaluate the impact of mental triggers on your email campaigns.

Examples of KPIs (Key Performance Indicators) Specific to Mental Triggers:

1. Abandoned Cart Conversion KPI:
   - Measures how many visitors who abandoned their shopping carts returned to complete their purchase after receiving a reminder with mental triggers, such as special discounts.

2. Social Sharing KPI:
   - Measures how many visitors share your content or products on social networks after being encouraged by social mental triggers such as "Share" buttons.

3. Newsletter Signups KPI:
   - Measures how many visitors sign up to your newsletter after being exposed to mental triggers like exclusive subscriber offers.

4. Survey Response Rate KPI:

- Measures the percentage of people who respond to surveys or questionnaires after being motivated by mental triggers, such as the promise of improvements based on feedback.

5. Repurchase Rate KPI:
- Measures how many customers return for additional purchases after having a positive initial experience based on mental triggers.

Adapting your KPIs according to your specific goals and mental triggers helps you more accurately assess the effectiveness of your persuasion strategies. Keep in mind that relevant metrics may vary based on your business type and marketing strategy.

5. Case studies of companies that have mastered mental triggers.

Case Studies of Companies that Mastered Mental Triggers:

1. Amazon – Social Proof Trigger:
- Amazon is known for its effective use of mental triggers, especially social proof. They incorporate customer reviews into their products, showing how many people have purchased an item and left

reviews. This builds trust with consumers as they see that others have already purchased and liked the product. Additionally, Amazon uses personalized recommendations based on a customer's past purchases, creating a sense of authority and personalization.

2. Apple – Curiosity Trigger:
   - Apple is a master at using curiosity as a mental trigger in its product launches. They keep secrets about new products until launch day, creating great expectation and curiosity among consumers. Apple's approach is to show just enough to make people curious, then reveal additional details at the right time.

3. Airbnb - Reciprocity Trigger:
   - Airbnb uses the mental trigger of reciprocity effectively, offering hosts the opportunity to leave reviews for guests and vice versa. This encourages people to be courteous and helpful during their stay, knowing that their reviews will affect your reputation. Reciprocity leads to more positive behavior and a more trusting community.

4. Coca-Cola – Emotional Trigger:
   - Coca-Cola has a long history of creating emotional ads that evoke feelings of happiness,

togetherness and celebration. They use emotional mind triggers to connect their drinks to special moments in people's lives. The famous "Hilltop" ad and Christmas campaigns are notable examples.

Lessons Learned and Best Practices:

1. Know Your Target Audience: All of these companies deeply understand their target audience and adapt mental triggers according to that audience's needs, values and desires.

2. Consistency: Implementing mental triggers consistently across all customer interactions helps build a solid brand image.

3. Test and Measure: All companies carry out rigorous testing to evaluate the effectiveness of their mental triggers. This involves measuring key metrics and adapting based on the results.

4. Mixture of Triggers: Companies often use a combination of mental triggers to create a more effective persuasive strategy. For example, Apple combines curiosity with scarcity in its product launches.

5. Transparency and Authenticity: Successful companies ensure that their mental triggers are authentic and not misleading. Customer trust is vital.

6. Monitoring and Feedback: Customer feedback is valued. Companies like Airbnb use review systems to maintain quality and reliability.

These case studies demonstrate how leading companies have mastered the art of using mental triggers to influence consumer behavior. The key to success lies in deeply understanding your target audience, maintaining authenticity, and constantly measuring results for continuous optimization.